Schubert Songs

John Watson

Schubert Songs

Schubert Songs
ISBN 978 1 76109 455 2
Copyright © text John Watson 2022

First published 2022 by
GINNINDERRA PRESS
PO Box 3461 Port Adelaide 5015
www.ginninderrapress.com.au

Contents

Preface 7
A Recital of Voices in Which Schubert is Addressed
   or is Recalled or Speaks Directly 9

Preface

Some of the incidents here are invented, some taken from the admirable volumes of Otto E. Deutsch: *Schubert, A Documentary Biography* and *Schubert, Memoirs By His Friends*, which are models of a method of biography all too rarely used. A few fragments derive from Dietrich Fischer-Dieskau's excellent *Schubert's Songs* and Charles Osborne, *Schubert and His Vienna*.

Schubert's music (which includes some six hundred songs) is, whether vocal or instrumental, essentially song-like, and the present title is intended to reflect this. To a degree – perhaps fancifully – I have also imagined each poem as a text for a song with accompaniment – some strophic, some in the manner of a recitative.

A Recital of Voices in Which Schubert is Addressed or is Recalled or Speaks Directly

In September of 1828

The composer was already indisposed,
And resolved upon a journey

To seek out Joseph Haydn's tomb
Beside which he lingered for some time.

To seek out Joseph Haydn's tomb
Beside which he lingered for some time,

He travelled down a curving path
And soon would see himself approach.

And, some weeks afterward, a meal

Of fish seemed vilely poisonous;
He threw down his knife and fork,

Retaining only lines and staves
And thereafter he scarcely ate

But sat up for several weeks
Correcting manuscripts until at last

He resolved upon a journey.

☐

Each evening towards dusk I walk,
My work complete by afternoon;
By then those leaping intervals

Which visit me have come and gone,
Have danced and left. And in their place,
More imprecise are dusk's faint cries:

The evening insects' zithering cry
The sky of wings invisible
The swallows scything in the field.

This is the pattern of my days:
The music of the spheres till noon,
And then, at dusk, the piping clouds.

❑

In one day he had written songs
In such a state of radiant

Exhilaration and delight,
He himself remarked to Spaun

While walking through the gilded fields,
His pockets filled with manuscript:

'I hardly knew it had begun
Before it hovered there entire.

Notes came to me like a cascade
Of poppies opening in their vase.'

❑

He seems to work in crowded company
Or solitude with equal ease. I know

That if you call on him during the day,
He says, 'Hello. How are you? Good!' without

So much as pausing in his flight
Across the fences of the staves. And yet

At times he is, I fear, distraught or lost,
Finding all substance vanished in the past;

And then he says, as if a ghost,
Familiar yet unseen, eluded him,

'I want to say with Goethe, "Who
Will bring me back an hour of that sweet time?"'

☐

Vienna in those happy days
Consisted of an inner part
Enclosed by walls, and to the north
The great Danube canal, its banks
A rampart. These enclosing walls
Were not yet those wide boulevards
The modern Ringstrasse would impose.

The real life of the capital
Took place between these narrow bounds
And further off were moats and towers
Which marked the suburbs. Even here
Whole districts still were pastoral
With woods and fields in miniature
In which the young composer walked.

☐

The summer of 1819 was
Amongst the happiest of all his days;

He called the sheltered vale of Steyr
'This inconceivably lovely place'

And in the house of Doctor Schellmann
Stayed for three months' growth of leaves.

To his brother Ferdinand he praised
'Eight young girls, all beautiful'.

☐

He told Spaun he could not afford
Ruled music paper. Spaun at once

Brought to his room many five-lined fields
For swallows to career and skim.

☐

There were several Franz Schuberts. One
Was a Dresden violinist, one

A folk singer of note, one
An officer in the cavalry

Famed for his collection of
Anthropomorphic beer steins.

At almost any given time
When one of these Franz Schuberts, say,

Was studying a lithograph
Of a pineapple on its spike

Or smiling at the lifelikeness
Of a woodpecker made of wood

Or warming cheese in a little pan
While snow fell distantly outside,

Or even when in a tavern
Two of these Franz Schuberts met by chance,

Their one immortal namesake was
Composing songs in which he had

Invented modulations none
Had ever entertained before.

☐

Therese Grob invited him
To sound the highest registers.

The song she sang had come to him
While walking in the laurel grove.

When first he saw and heard her sing,
Pale moonlight mixed with candlelight.

Her voice was on the high seas
And seemed to raise a sunlit sail.

☐

The Esterhazy summer residence
At Zseliz castle was a hundred miles
Far from Vienna and the Danube's arc.

Three children were his charges, one a boy
Of five, Marie and Karoline older and in flower
For whom he wrote the pianoforte duets.

Despite infatuation with the latter
Here he worked essentially alone
Hiding his love in bass and leger lines.

❐

When Karoline Esterhazy played,
The sun did something quite bizarre.
It singled out the piano vase
And drew a heart above her hair,

And pointing cried, *Look there! There!*

She wore a gown of yellow silk,
The yellow of the irises
Like intricately folded suns
Above the keyboard in their vase.

❐

There was, I have no doubt, a strain
Of vacillation in his character
Which gave his life that quality
Of flowering erratically

Like roses in profuse variety
Budding and falling on one branch.
The moment was his sole concern,
And burgeoning along a stem

His paradigm. We see him now
Composing in the midst of friends
At breakfast in the crowded coffee house,
A *sinica alba* rose opening to bees.

☐

When told that another Franz Schubert,
An astronomer, had recently discovered
A comet which thus acquired his name,

And that this comet was notable
For a curious obliquity in the tail,
The composer smiled and raised his glass

And said, 'Here's to the melody
Which, when it seems to approach a cadence,
Veers sideways into another key.'

☐

To friends a hundred miles from here,
Wrapped in the Danube's arms:
I am quite well,
        Heaven be praised,

And should be most contented here
If only I had you, my friends,
Schober and Kupelweiser,
        here with me.

But as it is, I long
Intolerably for home,
In spite of one attractive star,
        who alone

In this vast Esterhazy plain
Outshines the sun and writes
Along my heart's sleeve
        syncopated melodies.

☐

The *sinica alba* opens like a field
To swallows flying from the river wold;

Karoline Esterhazy holds a note
While someone turns the page.

A horse is grazing downwind. From the coach
An avenue leads on, through silver birch,

To almond blossom and a hidden gate.
And here a melody occurs complete

With its accompaniment. Cloud shadows pass.
The breeze brings petal flurries to the grass.

☐

The Esterhazy castle is
Not large but well appointed, and
The garden calm and quiet,
But for forty geese who follow me
And supplement discordantly
My modulations through the day.
I feed them and encourage them.
Small birds all harp on minor thirds
Unless on strange glissandos. Here
A groundsman is 'most musical'
And blows a German dance or two
Upon the flute, or strums a lute
Superbly. But, dear friends, I miss
Our Viennese duets and songs
And long to hear Frau Milder sing
– More beautifully than anyone –
Who still, I'll wager, cannot trill.
The chambermaid is pretty, and
Is often my companion now.
So far, I have been spared the task
Of dining with the family;
Instead I join her in the servants' hall.
My friends, write to me soon. You know
My only solace is to read
Your letters many, many times.

◻

Most Honoured and Esteemed Sir,
I am your privileged admirer,
Awaiting each published leaf and flower.

Theology and magnetism
And something of the life of plants –
These are my interests, as you see.

In music I am an amateur,
And yet I'd say your melody
And its refrain are like the flowers

Which twine together yet repel
Each other in a breezeless field,
Bright poppies wafting on the air.

◻

One morning in the coffee-house
Which was as dark as morning would allow
A waiter with a towel across his arm
Approached and enigmatically
Said, 'Sir, I think this message is for you –
Now, let me see. I think I have it here.
It doesn't make much sense, I fear:
Six Neapolitans desire to see you soon.
I think that's it. It's rather strange.'
'I know no one from Naples,' Schubert said.
'Well, just a moment. Look. It's here.
I wrote it on this café bill. Let's see.
Sausage and sauerkraut, four coffees
Three *zabaglione*, strudels each with wine.
Yes, here. I'll read it to you, Sir:
"Dear Franz," (that's you?) "the Danube weir
Is holding itself in readiness.
The sun is on the pool. Come soon.

A Neapolitan sixth awaits. Do not delay.
                Affectionately yours,

                              Spaun."

Who are these half dozen
Neapolitan gentlemen? I cannot help.
Yes, well. Before you go, Sir
Would Sir like another coffee cream?'

☐

This is how false legends grow:
Grillparzer said one day, 'You know,
I once saw Schubert sitting where
You now are sitting. A cigar

Dropped ashes on his coat. And so
Beethoven leaned across and blew
Them on the other's notebook there
And said, "Here is a theme."'

And yet, this pair of blazing stars
Had crossed but once in all those years,
(And even this a time for tears);
And Schubert did not smoke cigars.

☐

Amidst a plethora of minor Franz Schuberts:
From the Music Room of
Franz Schubert of Dresden:
'Illustrious Sirs,

                It is with indignation
That I have to inform you

That about ten days ago I received
Your esteemed letter enclosing
A manuscript setting of Goethe's Erl-King
Purporting to have been by me.
It is with the greatest astonishment
To which I may add annoyance,
Nay, outrage, that I have to inform you
That I am not the author
Of this worthless *cantata*
And that someone is misusing my name.'

☐

When Vogl called, Schubert had gone,
But, on the desk, there was a song
Composed on tiny paper scraps,
While music paper lay unused.

Just then the copyist arrived
And took these fragments. When, next day,
Vogl performed it, Schubert said,
'That isn't bad. Who is it by?'

☐

I do not quite recall the year.
Capus von Pichelstein had come
And brought a Schubert Rückert song
Stating his wish to accompany me
On the harp, his favourite instrument.
Capus at that time was estranged
From his fiancée and desired
To win her back by musical means.

And so, this very night, we went,
The cellist Merk, my humble self,
The violinist Schuppanzigh
And Schubert. Reaching Kahlenberg,
The hamlet where the Bertholds lived,
We waited for the last lights
To be extinguished. Then we played
The lilting *Trio* for violin,
Cello and pedal harp. I sang
A Schubert song *Sei mir gegrüsst*
And Schubert said, 'No one has sung
That song as you have done tonight.
You've brought tears to our eyes.'
And after other offerings
We went indoors where Frau Berthold
Provided light refreshments. Ah!
Midnight had come and gone before
We left. The pair were reconciled,
And Capus later married here
His Fraulein Marie von Berthold.
From this time onwards Schubert came
Quite frequently, and brought with him
Enchanting songs for me to sing.

❑

Herr Vogl in his later years
Was not averse to altering
The register or text of songs
Or even the melodic line;

Dramatic songs he made his own
By adding flourishes at will
If this might suit his purposes
Enhancing his performances.

At such times Schubert wryly said,
'That isn't bad. Who is it by?'

☐

A lady asked, while eating cake,
'Pray tell me: what is Schubert like?'

Schwind, in his devastating way,
Replied, 'A drunken cabby, I would say.'

While someone kinder smiled and said,
'He's like a hidden fountainhead,

A breeze that spirals in the wood
And lifts the leaves above the glade.'

☐

At Zseliz in the afternoon
As crowds pressed round the baritone
The Princess sensing his neglect
        Sought Schubert's side;

        But he replied,
'I'm happier to sit alone,
To hear the piano fade and see
The lilies in the windows bloom.'

☐

The Esterhazy family had
A young and humorous cat who would
Leap up and scatter music, and
Upset the swaying music stand,
Splash water from the crystal vase
Of purple orange irises.
Amused the Countess Karoline
Said, 'Even when he's lying down
He's accident-prone.'
And in Karoline's presence
I feel similarly erratic.

☐

When we see those publishers
Flying through Vienna's streets
Superb in their shining phaetons,
We understand the noble pride

Of the fine horses bearing them.
For like the steeds of Homer's gods,
They feed on pure ambrosia –
The immortal songs of Franz Schubert.

And yet those drivers should look down
From their lofty heights and see this Maker
Bending at the golden well
From which he draws these imperishable gifts.

☐

A row of silver birch in leaf
Between the coach and distant hill

Extends the road which turns at last
And vanishes below the crest;

Unique yet indistinguishable,
Each tree a flourish on its curve

That line is like the melody
Andante et espressivo

The coach appears to read at sight
While leaves shine in the glittering light.

☐

I always loved performing Schubert's songs;
But on this occasion something wonderful
Seemed to occur, in which the choice of song,
The place and time, the magic of the words
Were linked in unison or, rather, joined
In one long riband floating round our heads
The shape of Schubert's heavenly melody.

And now the evening was at hand. The church
Was cool and dark and yet the golden light
Fringed with the colours of the glass, framed us.
I sang with greater fervour than I'd known
And suddenly, at this coherence, tears
Ran down my cheeks and threatened several notes.
Such inexplicable joy might not return!

☐

Especially delightful were those evenings
Which the Imperial Chief Steward of the salt mines,
Hofrat Franz Ferdinand Ritter von Schiller,

Himself a capable musician, organised.
Then Schubert joined Nanette Wolf, the daughter of
Johann Nepomuk Wolf, municipal schoolteacher,

And she (Nanette) sang Schubert songs so beautifully
That he would modestly direct the applause to her.
Of course the audience, while generous, did not know then

That Schubert was with the immortals. Even Lenau
(And this some years still later) placed above him
The now forgotten composer Johann Rudolf Zumsteeg.

☐

In 1825 I took up lodgings
In the Landstrasse. This delightful house
In the Beatrixgasse has long since been pulled down.

While there I made one solitary excursion
Into the mountains in the August heat.
I climbed a glacier in Carinthia,

But did not shield my eyes with black gauze.
I also knocked my foot against a scree
Making it bleed. So, once back in Vienna,

I suffered inflammation of my eyes,
And when the wound in my foot broke out
I lay in scorching heat confined to bed.

There Schwind and Schubert came to visit me
And for a fortnight until I could walk
Distracted me with gossip, laughter and song.

☐

Arriving at the concert house
We passed through rows of blossoming trees
Each haloed still with swarming bees.

Schubert began to play
And as that blossom showered over us,
Each cascade seemed a productive hive.

☐

Hatwig who played the violin
Resided in the *Schottenhof,*
An ancient Scottish monastery
(Though *Scotia* stood for Ireland then),
And Schubert brought to him one day
Some sheaves whose ink was scarcely dry.

Sonnleithner owned the Gundelhof;
As Chief Judge at the Courthouse, he
Attained in 1828 with pride
The honour of the prefix *von.*
While Schubert songs which modulate
Outshine the honours of the State.

Before their deaths, within two years,
The Frölich sisters' total span
Was ten times Schubert's thirty-one,
Yet Schubert wrote six hundred songs.
His scattered notes across a page
Outlast the vastness of an age.

☐

The poet Grillparzer and he
Followed the stream. And eagerly

Pursuing in that sound a song

Grillparzer turned the corner first
And saw (stout Cortez at the coast)

The Frölich sisters frolicking.

Above them fell the waterfall,
A necklace of baroque pearl;

And later he could not explain
Why of these four he saw just one

His Katherina, with the sky,

Her parasol a descant, high
Above the running melody.

☐

Serene cantilenas rise
Above the waterfall's replies;

A pattern of descending thirds
Bears on the stream its eddying words.

This melody dissolves in sighs
Like clouds across late summer skies

But not before he draws up staves
And in their spray transcribes these waves.

❐

Sometimes when Anna Frölich sang
With Schubert raptly listening

No sooner had she finished when
He'd ask to hear it all again,

And then again and then again –

An aria from *Seraglio*
Or something from *Fidelio* –

He'd close his eyes without a word
And press his fingers to his head,

And when she stopped he'd smile and then
Ask her to sing it yet again.

❐

For the first and last time the two men
Who had lived as strangers in the same city

Met for a brief interval and spoke
In a curtained room in the company of others.

A week later Beethoven's death occurred,
Like rain falling on the whole world.

Schubert was one of thirty-six torch-bearers
Bearing this flame to its extinguishing cave.

☐

To my friends,
                Mayrhofer's *Solitude*
I have this minute just set.
The ink is drying on the page.

This *Solitude* is my delight.
Yet is it not an irony
That I should want
So much to share
This music with you and to wish
You here in Zseliz
Without whom everything is solitude?

☐

I direct you to domestic bliss.
Behold that bureau's inlaid panel doors
Those patines of bright gold, such *resonance!*
The decorative finds sheltered anchorage
In family life, a curtained drawing room.
There blossoms in the Beidermeier age
A kind of calm reclusiveness, where charm
And sensitivity are born. Beneath
The cloud of Metternich's paternalism,
People, denied a voice in public life,

Turn inwardly to vocalise their thoughts
And feelings, filial sentiments, the hush
Of hearth and cradle. So they cultivate
The parlour game, the sentimental salon,
The evenings at the piano for duets,
Democracy at home, the bright exchange,
The view of Nature as an analogue
For culture, form and order in their lives.
Behold harmonic waywardness within
A decorous and romantic sense of form,
And piano chords heard with the town hall clock.

☐

My father, a physician, was
In great demand. When I was seven,
We visited a mill in the woods.

The coach drive in rain seemed very long.
How much I would have liked to sip
A refreshing cup of creamy milk.

I waited for him in the parlour
And sipped a brimming cup of milk.
The maid laughed and showed me in a mirror

The white beads on my upper lip.
And nearby at another table
With bread and a glass of wine

A short and stout young man was seated
Staring into space, and sometimes
Glancing at the wet green window.

Years later when I saw a likeness
I knew that I was one of the few
Men living who saw Schubert live.

How I would like once again
To sip a cup of creamy milk
Beside him brimming with melody.

☐

Someone was calling from the garden.
Someone was seated at the piano.
A young lady was at the French doors,
Her hand holding the blind cords.

Someone
        produced the proposed poem.
He took the sheet and stood quite still
Perusing these lines. Someone called
From the garden. Someone else
Was leaving the piano. A young lady
Was sitting down to play.
                        Someone

Came in and said, 'That is the poem
We all considered you should set.'
And he said, as the garden shone,
'I've got it all, I think. It's done.'

☐

Grillparzer had written:
If from Kahlenberg you have seen
The country around you,
You will have understood
What I write and what I am.

What I write and what I am
Is therefore the outlying woods
And wide fields and vineyards
Encircling Vienna on every side,
The woods and the winding Danube.

☐

There is nothing more agreeable
Than the green countryside
After a hot summer day.
For this purpose the fields
Between Währing and Döbling
Seem to have been especially made.

In the mysterious twilight
With my brother Karl for company
I felt so happy and contented.
'How beautiful!'
I thought and exclaimed aloud
Standing still with enchantment.

Standing still with enchantment
I thought and exclaimed aloud,
'How beautiful!'

I felt so happy and contented
With my brother Karl for company
In the mysterious twilight.

☐

I hoped to talk and reminisce
With Schubert – just the two of us.
Alas, filling the coffee-house
Siebert the famous bass,

Who as we turned to leave in haste
Attached himself, would not desist.
Our only remedy was to walk
But Siebert still must talk,

And followed us into the hills.
We climbed past plunging rills
And could not ever shake from us
Siebert the famous bass.

Then Schubert said, 'Dear Siebert, sing
For us. For here, your voice will ring
With splendour in the mountain air
And we'll stand over there –

Just in the woods below this hill;
This should impart a magical
And dying fall to your fine voice.'
Siebert the famous bass

Consented and began at once
Long arias from this eminence
Which we left fading fast behind
As lightly we returned.

Siebert the famous bass
Now serenaded empty space
While we resumed our former place
With laughter, in the coffee house.

❑

I'll make you coffee. Here are coffee beans
And this most musical of all machines,
> My little mill.
> I lack only
> The fair maid.

I turn the handle thus and all the room
Is splashed and wet with heavenly perfume.
> I am content;
> My little mill
> Gives me ample grounds.

I turn the handle and the ratchet sings;
And from this sweet cacophony there springs
> A flood of melodies
> And so I thank
> My little mill,

For fragrance and each musical device
Which floats out in its noise – and then, of course,
>> The coffee which helps
>> Keep me awake
>> To write them down.

☐

A riotous yet lyrical duet;
And outside in the street another bout
Of blanket-tossing in the windswept light,
At which the subjects, briefly weightless, float,
Thrown up to hang at laughter's dizzy height
Against the moon where nothing else has weight.
Then bringing ale, the maid's swept off her feet,
And seated on the piano, still sedate
Amongst the brimming glasses she has brought,
She smiles like one remote, inviolate,
Acknowledging their cries. And yet a sight
Familiar and expected draws them out:
Schwind wears his billowing coat as black as night
And leaping in the raven-startling street
Performs his famed impression of free flight.

☐

Dear Ferdinand,
>> Today
Each oddity suggests a melody:

A neighbour climbed out on my balcony
And leaped to his because he'd lost his key.

A girl as pale as lily fields at dusk
Knocked timidly soon afterwards to ask

If I had seen a dove. I wished I had.
She sighed, and then we saw the very bird

Land on my balcony, while from the street
I heard a distant mandolin repeat

The selfsame tune I'd heard a week ago
And then neglected to write down. And so

I'm fully occupied – as you can see –
My head is swimming – brimming – happily.

☐

In a watercolour by Kupelwieser
The Excursion of the Schubertians

Twelve of their number crowd sedately
In a landau drawn by two horses.

Schubert stands considerately aside
In a token landscape which might be snow.

At about this time a giraffe was brought
To Vienna to great public astonishment

And hair styles *à la giraffe* flourished.
The craze for charades became a mania.

And despite the novelist Stifter's opinion
That a boiling kettle was as interesting

As a volcano, the theatre witnessed
Extravagances involving live cannon

Or live camels crowding the stage.
And yet the civic authorities

Desiring to be authoritative forbade
Dancing of any kind during Lent,

And police once raided a house
And prevented Schubert playing waltzes.

◻

A fondness for repetition
The 'observance of repeats' being crucial
To his attaining cohesion

Might be seen as a reflection
Of regularities in a world
Where innumerable repetitions

And repetitive innumerability
Are rife and are encountered, say,
Replete in the Vienna woods.

Here 'repeats of observances'
Is the rule generally observed
As in orchards seen from the coach

Or forests of silver birch
Arrow-flecked convict-white
Hastening to regroup as the coach

Trundles past the swinging open
Gate of rows. Even the sun appearing
Above an elegant coiffure of conifers

And spreading speckled warmth
On our faces and arms,
Despite its unexpectedness

When Rococo clouds have been
Intricately mannered over the valley
Before parting to reveal it,

Exemplifies the great principle
Of repetition in its habit
Of rising, sailing and setting.

The observance of repeats being crucial
To our calibration of the day
With dawn and noon and dusk

And heart and pulse beats
And the cooperative air repeated
In breaths and sighs, so

Irregularity becomes immediately
Exquisite simply by virtue
Of its departure from these networks

Like a fleece-goat tethered
And grazing ruminatively, freely
Over a field of buttercups.

The observance of repeats also
Augments what Schumann calls Schubert's
'Heavenly length', that is the sense

That an idea is being unrolled
Like a landscape by the eye
Looking along and below a horizon

At fields and patches of shade, crops,
Outcrops of rock and groves dazzling
In patches of shade as clouds move.

For then as the gaze returns
With affection to a certain herd, or creases
Or pleats in the hillside, or marks

And irregularities in the rockface
Scored there by ancient glaciers
So the lyrical prolongation

Of exquisite gatherings like folds
In the fall of the melody
May be encountered again

And again, the observance of repeats
Returning us to groves or a lake
Or a herd which seems to have moved

While retaining some familiar grouping
As the sun and clouds agree
To announce that noon has passed.

□

Schubert's tonality
Is as wonderful as star clusters
Burning and deliciously moving
In impalpable arcs
In the very reaches of space
Which they illumine and thus define
And Schubert's tonality is
As wonderful as star clusters
Shimmering in binary alternation
And beautiful in the night sky
As the mysterious trill which repeatedly returns
In the opening movement of the last sonata.
Schubert's tonality is as
Wonderful as star clusters
Strange and unanalysable,
As unpredictable as the fusion by which
Hydrogen spontaneously becomes helium.
As unclassifiable as the galaxies
Of star-forms of many kinds –
Red dwarfs, collapsed neutron stars,
black holes, pulsars,
Schubert's tonality is as wonderful
As star clusters
And as astonishing as the stars'
Consuming themselves to provide
the very substance
Of our own cellular translucent bodies.
So Tovey writes
Schubert's tonality
Is as wonderful as star clusters
And a verbal description of it
Is as dull
As a volume of astronomical tables.

At two a.m.
                the candle gutters
Violently as if it suffered too
And shared my pain,
                as if it too were buffeted
By those same winds of fortune. Ah!
Most enviable Nero!
                Would I had your power
To end all treachery with a violin.

❑

The swallows loop us in a coil
And draw us on across the field.
And casting us in their rondel
The swallows loop us in a coil.
Their wings dark as a tilting sail
Against the curved receding world,
The swallows loop us in a coil
And draw us on across the field.

❑

The swallows loop us in a coil
Of ribbons from the evening sky
Suggesting that the time comply
In a rondel *à l'hirondelle;*
And turning on a festive pole
Whose bands enswathe us in a sigh
The swallows loop us in a coil
Of ribbons from the evening sky.
As dusk takes us beyond the pale
They seem to fly more urgently:

As if they long at last to tie
And lead us inescapably,
The swallows loop us in a coil.

☐

Against the gathering of the cloud
Intent on bringing showers to bear
We hear
The ring dove's enharmonic leap.

Amidst the calm returning sun
Obliging, trembling cloud to clear
We hear
The ring dove's *Tierce de Picardie*.

☐

Looking at the photograph
The house in which Schubert was born,
Nussdorferstrasse 54,
We note that snow fell recently,

That some lies still in melting crusts
Across a parked barouche's hood.
But even had we travelled there
And stood outside that studded door

And peered in at the mullioned pane
The place would still seem difficult,
Resistant to our vain desire
To fill the street with reverent snow,

As difficult, unyielding, bare
As excavated walls in Troy
Beneath indifferent skies. There may
Not even be a piano here.

☐

Schellmann remarked, 'I sometimes feel
How strange it is that he
Seems not inhibited at all
By this Olympian art…'
(Someone was playing the *Hammerclavier*
And was approaching with devoted skill
The fearful and sublime cadential trills,

While Schubert, smiling, gazed from the window sill.)
Outside, a little girl
Was skipping blithely with a rope,
Then running with a hoop
Then turning cartwheels in the sunlit street.
He watched this bright cascade and heard as well
The fearful and sublime Olympian trills.

☐

Poor Siebert sang to empty space
Still teetering on the rugged peak.
And all around him echoing
Seemed masculine, heroic, bleak.

While Siebert's voice was fading at our backs
Schubert already found new branching tracks.

And in the wood we found a place
Where fern fronds opened to the sun;
While birds sang sweetly in the breeze,
And all the world was feminine.

As Siebert's hunting horn rang from the cliffs,
Schubert wore antlers through fresh clefs.

☐

A silky oak with cadmium flame
Against a screen of conifers,
Superb above a suppliant stream,

Recalled the *prima donna* at
The opera, when we reached our box,
Just as the curtain opened on

Act II: The Countess enters Right,
And stands above our wooded stream
Magnificent, imperious,

And does not move. But when she sings,
The tree puts out its burnished bracts
And all our forest floor seems mute.

Enter the Count. She favours him
As well with fortunate regard
As with this liquid gold glissade,

And in his happiness the Count
Rotates a sundial on the stage
And leaves it thus, then exits left.

Then, while we felt delicious doubt
At whether chords supporting her
Were moving to the minor key,

Our box received a visitor:
Decolletage, pale powdered skin,
Eyes like a clear cerulean sea.

She took her seat; her lorgnette glowed.
The countess reached a long-sustained,
profoundly eloquent high C.

❐

Our New Year's Eve festivities
Went well, I think. Towards midnight
We went to Mohn's. Soon everyone's
Best sweethearts were proclaimed in toasts;

Bruchmann and Kupelwieser sang,
Eichberger could not be restrained,
Toasting *his* sweetheart several times.
Schubert took over the piano.

A soprano seemed to materialise.
A galleon sailing through the crowd,
She ventured beyond high seas.
A glass shattered. The year chimed twelve.

❐

This reviewer deems himself entitled
To speak in greater detail
About the unwarrantably strong
Inclination to modulate again and again

With neither rest nor respite,
Which is a veritable disease of our time
And threatens to grow into modulation mania
To which even famous composers succumb.

Such modulatory exercises may
Indeed have their uses
But only for students of harmony –
For all composition pupils begin

By being wild and foolish but, later,
Modulate less and less, from which
We may conclude that such aimless straying
Is merely the regrettable inability

To remain in one place at one time.
Herr Schubert writes creditably but in a manner
Which lacks inner unity, order and regularity,
And in which eccentricities proliferate.

☐

At the *Snail,* Spaun and Spaun's betrothed,
The Ottenwalts and Schwind. We danced,
I for much of the time with Frau von Ottenwalt.
Then to Bogner's where we sat till after twelve.
Schubert and my brother played duets. It was
Two o'clock before we left, in the seventh heaven.

To the *Partridge*. Schwind and I talked.
The Minister of Finance and his second wife were there.
To the ale-house of the *Burgundian Cross*,
Where however one cannot smoke. So we adjourned
To the *Snail* where it was so noisy
That we went on to the *Partridge*. Despite eighty
Coffee-houses in Vienna it is sometimes difficult
To find one which is both quiet and convivial.
In the morning by express coach to the Ottenwalts'
Where we enjoyed a Schubertiad. Supper, then a ball.
To *The Wolf Preaching To the Geese*. Rather dull.
To the *Partridge*. At twelve thirty the Ehlers
And Jérôme, who was tipsy, arrived.
We all went on to Bogner's coffee-house
Where Jérôme vomited. To Leibenfrost's coffee-house.
Braun, Dr Hörwater and Schubert were there.
Songs, the ink scarcely dry on the page.
At the tavern (the *Monastery*) there was such a to-do
With the unmannerly hostess and her husband also,
That we resolved not to go there again. Jérôme sardonic.
In the morning Enk fetched me to the *Partridge*
Where I played eleven rounds of skittles.
Repeatedly I struck the ball without it once
Dislodging a single cone. *Enk jubilant*. Afterwards
To the *Snail* where Schwind and Bayer
Were making drawings from a given net of dots,
While Schober composed a poem using
A given list of words and Schubert
Devised a German Dance from a given set of notes.

Still at the *Snail* where Spaun tried to do a trick
Using a pipe stem. He made a pass with it,
The upper part remained in his hand
While the other piece flew at the head of a guest
In the next room. Home at midnight.
After wooing Netti, Schwind returned to Bogner's
In despair over a mishap resulting in
His black frock coat being torn. Schubert
Could not help laughing, but good-naturedly.
Schwind was betrothed, but in October the engagement
Was broken off. To Schobers'. We read Kleist.
Rain forced the postponement of a drive into the country.
To the *Partridge*. Schwind behaved badly towards Sauter,
Who acted generously in the circumstances.
Enk began a race in the street.
Schubert played splendid four-hand pieces
With my brother until after midnight.

❑

Amongst the touching scenes at Linz
Were those in which, when Vogl sang

And Schubert played, a concert had
To be abandoned or delayed

For after several sad songs
The ladies had dissolved in tears

And even the gentlemen were seen
To struggle to contain themselves.

❑

The last Schubertiad at Linz
Was held at Spaun's. The following day

Schubert and Vogl parted company,
Vogl to go to Italy,

And Schubert in a hired coach
To travel back to Vienna,

The journey taking three days
Through countryside which meant so much to him,

And which he would not see again.

◻

Up to its flanks in the pond
The horse strikes the water with its hoof.

The single tree once flowering
Is now almost unseen against the hill.

The grass is long and dry
Between long rows of apple trees in leaf.

The last blossom fallen,
The year turns to the hard matter of fruit.

The coach rounds the curve.
Inside he writes across hand-ruled lines.

◻

Beneath the cedar's lilac flower
Still hang bright pods of autumn gold.

When you are elsewhere, all the world
Seems frozen, seized with here and now

And so the seasons cannot part
Nor quite disintricate themselves

And every melody delays
Its resolution to an end.

Beneath the cedar's lilac flower
Still hang bright pods of autumn gold

Because the seasons cannot part
Nor quite disintricate themselves

And every melody delays
All cadences till you return.

☐

The rowan fruit, remarkably
Articulate, serene and bright
        Recalls your lips
        When, having sung,
You smiled and bowed,
        Then sought me with your eyes.

For, having sung *The Rowan Tree,*
Your lips recalled its glowing fruit
        One evening, when
        With lightning, dusk
Competed for a sieve of falling light.

☐

The mill wheel is already distant
As if it were the mill and not we who travelled.

Trees in new growth still tightly furled
Have arranged themselves so as to cover the slope.

The air is filled with the most leisurely
Drift of seeds following each other over fences.

The profusion of trees and air and insects
Seems out of all proportion to the needs

Of anyone travelling here along the river's edge.
The birds for instance have learnt to ignore everything.

❐

The minor third glints with the sword
Of bright, unstable dissonance;
Its fourth harmonic flourishes
Three octaves higher in the clouds,
An anvil-clanging major third.

This armoury he loves to bear.
On each flecked grove, each line of hills,
Each coach view catching the canal,
The sun moves in and out of cloud
To alternate in light and shade.

❐

From the coach
The evening sky was litmus pink.

From the coach
The ordered forest walked away
And variously kept pace with us.

As evening fell
We heard those birds which sound like bells
Who live in steeply sloping woods
And when they sing cannot be seen.

The coach descended by the pass
Where these birds drew about themselves
The ribbons of an evening sky.

From the coach
The evening sky turned Prussian blue.
And in the darkening coach
He still added notes to the stave.

❑

I am convinced, my friends, that happiness
Is often little more than this:
Conjunctions of the simultaneous.

You smile, and yet you must recall
The happiness we felt this afternoon
When in the coach we came upon

The sudden field of lavender in bloom
Just as we sang that lilting song
On sheets torn from the lining of a hat.

And as we watched the harvesters
And slowly crossed a shallow glittering stream
A lady's glove fell from the door.

Then leaning out we sang more boisterously.
The lavender was just a haze
The distant harvesters were clambering bees.

And so, my friends, such things conspire
To overlap. They float deliciously
And turn on the uncertain stream.

☐

In fertile watering-pastures between poplars
A cow rises on its elbows
Like a writer bending over a lectern.

Billowing towards them, profuse orchards
Contribute a tasselled air
To the immense air of fruition

Already sweet with cedars flowering.
Fecundity is a pollen
As inevitable as these several airs.

And, as fruitful as these, Schubert appears
In crowded company, to confound
Every expectation of sonata form

By the advocacy of impingements,
Affectionate embraces, and by indications
That he will not plough these fields.

❏

Opium poppies grow in the carriageway
Where horses have recently grazed.

After a dry winter aniseed plants
Are growing again towards their dry stems;

These seeding straws divide and divide
Like delicate genus and species charts.

Hedges of these fine lace struts
Suggest his melodies dividing and dividing,

The leaves clambering towards their branching stems,
His passionate pursuit of them.

❏

Below the glacier we sat
At tables in the glistening sun
And drank the health of Schubert's Muse.

Just as the glacier (you said)
Adheres against its scouring rock
And slides and groans and writes and sighs –

Imagine this impacting force
Accelerated to a waltz
Peculiarly Viennese

And here you have that strange device –
The enharmonic interface
Round which his melodies cohere.

And even as we faced the sun
And each recharged and raised his glass,
Spring melted ice and fresh streams ran.

☐

The coach stopped. The horses grazed.
The oak leaves uniformly pale,
Their shades were cloaks beneath each tree.

An inn was hidden in a lane
Beneath arpeggios of leaves;
Indoors the gloom seemed welcoming.

A fortepiano in a room
With several notes which would not sound
Excited him inordinately

As if one might negotiate
Several paths across a stream
With widely scattered stepping-stones.

☐

The house where Schubert died
Again in snow, with barriers

Between the footpath and the street,
(With a van parked inside this rail)

Offers one strangely obvious,
Symbolic and deliberate thought:

Of eighteen upper windows closed
        One is opened wide.

☐

We went to Bogner's coffee house
(In those days in the *Singerstrasse*)
And Fraulein Rinna von Sarenbach
(With flowers in her hair) was there
And Netty Hönig pale and fair
(For whom Schwind bore a smoking torch).
With her we went (one afternoon
As rain came) to the skating rink.
And one day we were drinking wine
And heard of Schubert's death. Kübeck
Who later took his own life
Brought me a lock of Schubert's hair.

☐

Poor Schwind and I could not believe
Our friend had left so suddenly.

Only a week before, he spoke
Of harmonies as yet unheard:

All these he carries to his rest.
And Schwind and I could not believe

That he would be with us no more.
Thus for a time either of us

Would gladly in his place have died –
An understandable conceit,

Since, from the world, all harmony
Had passed into harmonious spheres.

☐

A murmuration of starlings,
An exaltation of larks,
A cheer of Schubertians
Set out to see the lavender harvested,
A haze of lavender.

A charm of finches,
An ostentation of peacocks,
A descant of Schubertians
Leaned at the piano singing new songs,
A profusion of songs.

☐

Approaching the confluence of Lethe and the Styx
Charon is startled to hear
Strange music from the tourist deck.

Impulsively and inexplicably
He turns inshore
And soon the ferry eddies in pleasant shallows.
A warm Danube sun comes and goes.

Viennese pastries and an exceedingly light strudel
Accompany revels. The same persistent music
Which has already swayed his purpose

Echoes across the stream so liltingly
That, slowly turning, they drift backwards,
And are in danger of running aground. It is
The song: *To Be Sung On the Water.*

◻

That last November's calendar
Is richly bare:

The meal of fish thrust aside,
Living without food, sitting in bed;

He makes an appointment
For lessons in counterpoint

But soon there begin
Those modulations which will not return
To any known key.

◻

Ferdinand, interpreting
His brother's wishes, saw to it
That Schubert's grave would be

Almost at Beethoven's side;
But by an oversight
Two others lie between them.

And so it is that we are gathered here
Where moss and thistle stifle lavender
To speculate upon the extraordinary

Experience of the spirits of these two
Who lie between, who rise and yet return
To hear the Olympian dialogue which fills

And still overflows the air, still brimming here.
We may imagine these astonished ghosts
Drawn back, foregoing their Elysia

To hear faint echoes of those radiant
Descriptions of the universal, here
Spelt out on keyboards once, still resonant.

☐

The events of those last tragic weeks
Distressing as they are to me still
Contain one indisputably remarkable
And startling fact
Which taken in the context of the rest
Cannot but win amazement.

Consider: two weeks before the end
There is the incident of the fish,
After which he ate little food again.
And yet he still corrected manuscripts.
A week later, that is, one week
Before his death,
To make good perceived deficiencies
He requested an appointment with Sechter
For lessons in counterpoint.

▫

When Schwind brought Schubert to my house
I entertained them with a verse
Romantic but preposterous;
We sang and played duets, and then

Repairing to the coffee house
Continued long into the night
With talk of music, life and love.
When one is young there is so much to tell
That time is never long enough
(And art is inexhaustible).

In short, our ship of life sailed on
With all its sails outbillowing
Until it foundered on the reef
Of Schubert's death.

And after forty years had passed
And Schubert's statue was unveiled
I stood with Lachner (not, alas, with Schwind)
And we recalled those sunlit days
As if they'd been *fantasias.*

☐

Dismembered Orpheus carried downstream,
Still singing, for so many centuries
That he has wearied of his repertoire,

Finds himself in shallows. The water is clear.
Beneath it can be seen remnants
Of decorous Beidermeier rooms. He hears

Strains of a regenerative music, harmonies
Carried on the water which reawaken his
Passion. It is *To Be Sung On the Water.*

☐

www.ingramcontent.com/pod-product-compliance
Lightning Source LLC
Chambersburg PA
CBHW070338120526
44590CB00017B/2930